DON'T WAIT TO LIGHT THE CANDLES

ALSO BY ALLIE MICHELLE

Explorations of a Cosmic Soul

The Rose That Blooms in the Night

The Words Left Unspoken

Legends of Lemuria

DON'T WAIT TO LIGHT THE CANDLES

ALLIE MICHELLE

ISBN-13: 978-0-7783-0673-3

Don't Wait to Light the Candles

Park Row Books
22 Adelaide St. West, 41st Floor
Toronto, Ontario M5H 4E3, Canada
ParkRowBooks.com

HarperCollins Publishers
Macken House, 39/40 Mayor Street Upper,
Dublin 1, D01 C9W8, Ireland
www.HarperCollins.com

Printed in U.S.A.
26 27 28 29 30 LBC 5 4 3 2 1

For the women whose spirits
are a flame in the dark.

DON'T WAIT TO LIGHT THE CANDLES

There is this old saying, "Don't wait to light the candles."

Meaning, *don't wait to seize the beauty in front of you.* When a miracle knocks, and you find yourself standing in the doorway of an answered prayer, cross the threshold and *light the candles.* Maybe Skepticism and Hope fight for the last word in your mind as you try to wrap your arms around the possibility of a dream come true, but the fear of loss cannot stop us from discovering just how brightly we can burn.

Tell me the heart is irrational
And I'll tell you we were never meant
To ration our love for one another

Writing isn't my career
It's my way of saying,
For the tender blink of an eye
I saw you,
I saw all of you
And you were magnificent
Let me capture a glimpse of you with my pen,
So one hundred years from now
The world will have a window of beauty
To look through and know
A miracle like you existed.

Roses bloomed from my eyes when I was born
they say I've been blind to reality ever since,
but I think love is the only time we ever see rightly
and knowledge without heart
is like thorns without a flower.
this tongue learned poetry
before acceptable conversation,
before I trapped myself as a muse
instead of growing wings from my humanity.
All the exhausted women I have been sigh in relief.
Are we done?
Are we done trying to be everything now?
Yes, I tell them,
we are done.
I dance alone in my room,
the most beautiful moments of my life
happen without a witness . . .
the unknown like fresh oxygen
to my heaving chest,
because happily-ever-after
happens when we choose to see beauty
where others say there is none.

I have known women who have given up every comfort to dance alone under the night sky, unbothered by watchful eyes. Women who have stolen moments from their busy lives just to create—to sit at the pottery wheel and feel worlds of clay spin beneath their fingertips. I have known women who put on red lipstick to write and seduce the muse. I have known women who have sacrificed their sanity, clawed tooth and nail to not just climb toward success but disrupt the system all together with a wicked grin on their face. I have known women who have said, "To hell with your timelines and pressures," who have chosen a quiet life of growing herbs in the woods with wild, unruly hair. I have known women who have tipped their head back and howled in triumph as they gave birth, bringing life into the world while fighting an illness. I have known soft women and strong women and beautiful women and smart women. Women who have walked through the hell within themselves and emerged with a fire in their eyes, knowing heaven was in their wild hearts the whole time. Women who remind me what it means *to be a woman.*

Keep your defiant joy.
Keep your stubborn hope.
Keep your unyielding wonder.
Keep those childlike eyes you look at the world
   through—
they are not childish, but a rebellion against despair.
Keep your heart that tears but never breaks.
Keep the fingerprints the world has left on it.
Keep the stretches of sorrow, and the moments that split
   open in ecstasy.
All of it, all of it, all of it!
Nothing worth keeping can never be taken,
so keep the miracle of your life with you.
Let it spill over and water everywhere you go,
   every soul you touch . . .

I smile at the way your presence rewrote
every tragedy in my bones.

I am swept up in the current again,
yielding to tumbling rapids
as they wear away at my sharp edges
there is nothing to hold on to but
t r u s t
I hope everyone knows
the joy of such tenderness
I hope everyone lets these waters break against
everything they are not
I asked the river if she fears the day she will become
    the sea
the two of us laughed as we were carried
toward the spectacular unknown
I kiss the sea salt on
my smiling lips
and d i s s o l v e

I beg of you, don't forget that your life is meant to *SING*. When you feel bogged down by invisible chains that say you can't, you really shouldn't—rip away those bondages with sharp teeth and let freedom dribble from your chin. They tell you freedom is doing whatever you want, but what is freedom if not the radical surrender to life? We don't need more heroes in capes. We need holy bandits. People who dance when the earth rumbles and quakes beneath them. People who carry keys between their teeth so the words they speak unlock those bolted prisons within you. *What is a free soul, but someone who acts with so much heart that everything they do is a sacred rebellion?*

Sometimes, the greatest intimacy is born
From unflinchingly looking at your lover's fragments
  and saying,
"I have spent my life looking for a mosaic just like you . . ."

Last night I wrapped my rib cage around the world
and lit eight billion candles
in the cave of my heart
the stars grew jealous of their light
the way the flames flickered and danced
with embers of transformation
no one survives this earth unchanged
but I have begun to love the graveyard
as much as the garden
to string my memories like beads of prayer
on a necklace I can always touch
To remind myself
how wonderful it is,
just to be with each other.

Steal your beauty back from the world. Walk in this animal skin like every curve and edge was crafted from an impossible miracle, because it was. Gulp down that first breath in the morning and remember this body is *yours, yours, yours.* Yours to find pleasure in. Yours to dance in. Yours to listen to the pain of and nurture. Not yours *if* you bring enough to the table. Not yours if you bend far enough into the shape they desire.

Yours.

We have to steal back our joy. Don't let them convince you that you will be on the edge of madness if you feel it all. The walls of your heart are wide enough to contain the seven seas—you will not drown in your own emotional tides. Every day, the world will knock the crown from your head. *You have to steal it back.* Forge it with poetry, with song, with prayer, with dance—craft it again and again until your hands blister. Steal back your wildness, because we can no longer exhaust our aching hearts trying to belong to the world.

There is a species of bird with bones so fragile,
they've taught themselves to sleep in the sky.
I know a thing or two
about hollow skeletons and unyielding wings.
I know a thing or two
about ending the search for a place to rest your head,
telling Gravity to come back another day,
because you've earned a feather of steel
for every time you've crash-landed.
It has taken a thousand shatterings
to become this whole.

Moments are like fireflies.
We writers try to catch them in a jar,
Race barefoot through open fields
Grasping at time like we can freeze it.

I am still standing alone in that empty meadow
Trying to give voice to ordinary things.
Heaven is the way the oak trees smell before
seven in the morning
And hell is the days
I am not awake to notice.

I sometimes hear thunder crack the sky open
Only to realize it is my own heartbeat
This soft heart that longs to love unguarded
To let lightning strike my tongue so my smile
Is a north star in the night

Follow the joy of ordinary things
Only then will you be able to cry with the rainfall
Run wild with the wind
Burn brightly with the sun
And lay all the tired, aching versions of you to rest in
the soft earth.

Loosely, loosely, loosely. Hold it all loosely. It is excruciating when you grip so tightly life has to pry you finger by finger away from what doesn't belong to you. You cannot keep something that isn't meant to be kept. Not a person, a dream, or a place. The greatest act of love can be taking a break from what we love until it feels like a resounding *yes* again. When your hand is shaking, knuckles white with fear, there is no room in your palm to hold what *is* yours. Brave is the person who lets life in all the way, knowing one day they will have to give it back. *Loosely, loosely, loosely.* Why fight the current, when it is carrying you to wonderful places beyond your wildest imagination?

I cannot say, "I love you,"
Until I've met the darkness in your heart
Shaken hands with the shadows your soul casts
And woven a welcome mat for all the monsters inside
to know they have a home.
I cannot say, "I love you,"
Until I've studied the stained glass of your spirit
Marveled at the rich colors and patterns
Forged by every tragedy you turned into beauty.
I cannot say, "I love you,"
Until I learn to hear beneath the locked jaw,
and listen for the words you swallowed
in the name of survival.
I cannot say, "I love you,"
Unless I'm willing to be a sanctuary
strong enough to contain without confining,
To help you laugh your way out of the dark,
Until you see the stars again.
I cannot say, "I love you,"
Until happily-ever-after ends
And that gorgeously messy,
Frighteningly honest now begins.

Hope is not for the naïve. She is the final lantern carried through the storm. Hope doesn't wait for dawn to break—*she is the ember that refuses to die.* Hope doesn't clutch onto her last shred of certainty, waiting for life to prove trustworthy. She gives life her trust, palms open against all reason. Hope doesn't demand her path be revealed. She knows that when the road ahead disappears, she is walking her destiny. Hope is the resilience of the human spirit. She doesn't fear the fall. She knows the taste of dust, the sting of scraped knees, and that defiant heart that rises *again, and again, and again.*

We're taught life is linear—that everything resolves itself into neat little bows. Until one day, you're on a plane laughing with a man you thought would be your husband, who is now your best friend. Until your mother casts off her pearls and moves off-grid to the woods to fire Hula-Hoop. Until your friend tells you she's had a vital organ removed but has decided to become a professional horseback rider all the same. *Until, until, until.* That word is the only truth we have.

Take the silent prayers from my lips
and return them to me in poetry.
Reach through my skin and bones
and touch that beating place
where love and death and chaos meet.
Feel the center of my sorrow,
string it into a melody
and give this world a symphony.
On the days you feel bitter from swallowing
  life's cruelty,
walk through the garden of my mind
and taste the joyous honey of my memories.
Let's not talk of tomorrow,
there is too much beauty to look after . . .

My mother told me I am the first woman of
my bloodline
to stand on my own two feet
without reaching for a man for security.
Instead of the pride I should have felt for being a
girl boss
all I felt was the privilege of my time period sink
into me . . .

I felt the grief of my ancestors,
generations of women who were the invisible hands
weaving their husband's dreams
silently praying one day they may get to live out
their own,
because being a digital nomad or an entrepreneur
was hardly an option for them when they had mouths
to feed, unequal pay,
and the right to choose didn't exist.

When people ask me what my purpose is
all I want to say is,
"To make my bloodline proud."
All I want to say now is,
"I remember them."

I light a candle for those who came before me
because they paved the path I now walk.
We talk about generational curses
like all we inherited were heirlooms of trauma,
but what about the gifts they gave us?
What about the legacy that flows in our veins?
One day, I'll say to my future daughter,
"Baby, you stand on your own two feet,
but just know that you will never be alone,
because beneath them are the shoulders of every
ancestor who walked before you."

We were two magnets that separated ourselves
Just so we could feel how pleasurable it was
To finally come together.
His fingertips felt like electricity on my skin,
And I wonder if separation was God's way
of keeping lightning from burning us both.

I've learned that grief is a sneaky bastard who doesn't tell you when he is coming to visit, but that it's best to always let him in. I've learned that laughter reveals a person. There is the bubbling laughter of a child and the hopeful laughter of lovers and the dark laughter of survivors. I've learned that tears of joy and sorrow look different under a microscope, like they're waiting for someone to decipher the tale as to why they formed and fell. I've learned I can only truly understand that which I have the nerve to love. *I wonder what else I'll learn, what other beauty I'll find in this wild and wonderful world.*

How does a woman fill the chasm of longing
that carves its way through her?
She dances on her own fault lines,
Celebrating the earthquake of imperfection
Because every tremor
She once feared would undo her
Is a gift—
The hands that break apart
Her false sense of self.
Like stone wrapped in silk,
She will always find the strength it takes to be soft.
Paradise was never lost,
but tenderly resting in her
own unyielding heart . . .

It is a lucky thing to be the one who loved. Apathy cannot step forward with the tight shoes of "cool." Kick them off! Every blister is an emblem of courage. We will not escape the labyrinth of human suffering by caring less. Love is our map, but it directs us into the open and dares us to stay. Yet to reveal ourselves is to be a seed split open—only in breaking does real life grow. Our very existence becomes an offering of nourishment. So be the one who loves. What could be more lucky than a heart without edges?

Everything worthwhile risks embarrassment. Making art until you hone your craft? *Embarrassing.* Pushing your body's limits, wobbling awkwardly until you find your strength? *Embarrassing.* Learning a new language and sounding like a two-year-old? *Embarrassing.* Saying, "I love you," for the first time? *The greatest risk of all.*

Leaning into what we love may feel like a massive risk, but I say it's a massive risk *not* to. The world is a bizarre place to reside right now. Robots are making art, people are personal brands, and our food is engineered to outlive us. We see horrific videos of war one second, and then a flying chipmunk the next on the same platform. What else is there to do but love the world? *Love it unbridled. Love it beyond your comfort. Love it with embarrassing pride.*

I will love you if I never see you again,
Just as I loved you when I saw you every moment.
I will love you when your face is muddled by memory,
And all I can recall is the sound of your laugh.
I will love you if we make new memories,
And I once again hear my favorite song
As I listen to the *thump-thump* of your heart.
I will love you if you marry someone else,
And support you always from afar.
I will love you if you one day marry me,
and that tattoo on your hand can again mean more
    than a scar.
I will love you wherever you go,
No matter how far.
Because you are as intimately a part of me
As the air that I breathe.
And if one day I am to see you
And you've built a whole new life:
Kids of your own,
Books you've written,
And a beautiful wife,
I will smile at you and nod,
Because I will know

That our love was the foundation we both stand on
And no amount of time or space
Could possibly erase
The home I have carved out for you
In my heart.
And though, "I love you,"
Became, "I have to leave now,"
It was only because I knew
That we wouldn't become
Who we were meant to,
If we stayed together
But I promise, through it all I
will love you forever.

I don't know anything at all. Except for how to make time drip like honey—slow and thick, each moment warm in amber. Sunlight on skin. Paint between my fingers. The kind of kiss that makes me feel immortal. Sliding in socks on hardwood floors.

I don't know anything at all. Except for how to be lost. The way a path can stretch on for miles and it feels like you'll disappear in a forest of brambles. I know about tender, aching feet and how the only way to complete an impossible journey is one step at a time.

I don't know anything at all. Except for how to feel like I belong. To look up at the stars that shine like a river of silver, letting me drown in their beauty.

I don't know anything at all. Except for these words, this pen. *You. Me.* And this precious little time we are given.

The question of being human is not, *"How will I ever find a way out of my pain?"* but, *"What beauty will I make from it?"*

I am learning what it means to occupy this body
five feet and seven inches of untold stories
I am learning what it means to time travel to my
frozen selves,
we're going home, I tell them as I melt the ice.
I am learning what it means to quit acting in the play
of a perfect woman
and breathe into my belly like every inhale is a
reminder
that I am my own center of gravity
every exhale a refusal to spend my life
flattening my soft curves into a caricature
I am learning what it means to be a woman animated
from within
these swirling hips shake free of everything the world
calls me
a dancing woman doesn't just draw eyes,
she changes visions.

Make a friend of your lover, not a god. If you make a god of them, you will be swept away by wings of infatuation and fly so far off the ground the sun will blind and scorch you. You will only make love to a sparkling fraction of who they are, discarding the rest. If you make a god of your lover, you will one day make a demon of them too. The play will run out of script, and both of you will be revealed to be mortal again. Yet, if you can fall in love with the mortal, giving just enough space and warmth for someone to try on their own skin, your love will do exactly what it needs to: *transform you both*. It will encourage your humanity, your strength, your wildness, and above all—your truth.

I don't need a man who has a way with words—just one who means them.

Heartbreak and death have the same address . . .
except the person you love is still
walking around in the world
half family and half stranger
I suppose the only danger is regret,
going over every memory from the moment you met
wondering: *how did we get here?*
to the point when I couldn't hear
all of the signs screaming at me
until one day I blinked and
I'm waking up in the middle of the night
reaching for your warm skin
unable to tell where you end and I begin
but there is no you,
no *us*,
it's just me,
gasping for air as I drown in our memories
even standing among our ruins
I can't help but appreciate
all that we built . . .

I am in the middle. Aching feet from climbing snow-capped mountains. Needles in my lungs from swimming in glacier lakes. Tangled hair from dancing through what I can't find words for. Catching poems with a butterfly net. A heart that constantly tears but never breaks. I laugh until I cry and I cry until I laugh because *no feeling is final.* Life doesn't offer periods on the ends of sentences—we are all in the glorious and wonderfully messy middle.

If you're loved by a poet
you should know—
we will feel everything, and say nothing . . .
unless it's a poem.

Our words may not save the world,
but they could change your view of it.
We'll forget to arrive on time,
but we'll remember the look in your eyes
the first time you laughed loud enough
to crack open the sky.

We'll forget our keys and that important work meeting
but remember the scent of you years after you're gone.

Like bonfire smoke,
our love lingers long after it has been washed away,
but we'll never ask you to stay.

Instead, we'll use our longing as ink,
capturing the miracle of you with our pen,
so you'll always know—
the small, ordinary things you do are like
gravity to the ones who love you.

I believe in the in-between moments. Cooking to Louis Armstrong. Sitting on the counter while my best friend applies her makeup, talking about her new crush. Handwritten letters. Writing books on my staircase despite having an adequate desk. The color green. The way the sound of the piano is like an earthquake that shakes awake the slumbering parts of my heart. Howling into the canyon until the coyotes howl back. There's nowhere to get to, not really. Just a handful of in-between moments to grasp hold of like a dandelion, blowing our wishes back into the wind that we get to live more of them.

The silence between lovers is loud
Tell me,
When you close your eyes
Do you see the footprints I left
Dancing across your mind?
Tell me,
Does anyone read
Your body like their favorite book,
Losing themselves in your pages?
Tell me of how you grasp
The farthest-reaching star
And offer it in the smallest of gestures.
Tell me,
Don't tell me,
My ears are trained to hear
The words left unspoken . . .

Some days I feel like a guest in my own life,
Too afraid to sit on the furniture.
Until my loved ones kick down the door.
They rip open the drawers,
Clothes flying,
Their laughter shattering
The flawless mirror of silence.
I watch them as if through a window,
And see the divine mess
We make of each other's lives.

There will be years ahead of quiet.
Of stainless rooms,
And a too-perfect house.

My mind will replay their chaos
Like a jukebox of treasured memory,
My heart will long for the perfection
I once mistook for a flaw.
A house is not a home,
A body has no heart,
Without the fingerprints
We leave on each other's lives.

We talk about high value men and women as though
There is a scale sharp enough to measure a soul

As though a checklist could ever replace the moment
Someone flips your world in a single sentence

For the way your spirit falls silent
At the sound of their voice
And their eyes are equal parts
A prayer and a challenge
When they drink you in.

There is no standing in society
That can overpower the power of two people
Who met on a one-in-a-million chance
But would have lived a million lifetimes
Just to find each other again.

Tell me of your greatest love,
And then tell me

If they checked off your boxes,
If they could even fit in your boxes.
Or if their heart was so large it tore through
Everything you thought you wanted
But handed you what you always needed.

I see Death at the backyard fence,
waving me over.
I place a hand on my heart and bow,
"I'll walk willingly with you,
but will you gift me one more second? Just one."
"Just one," he agrees.
Like even he wants to see the way I'll spend my
last second.

I slip back inside,
and grab your hands
silently pulling you into a dance
beneath the open sky

Call it the writer in me,
but I always feel a story ending
before the final period is inked on the page.

I breathe you in,
your hand on my waist like a violin
"Play me one last time," I want to say
The strings quiver
Drawing tears at the sound.

One last dance
We're twirling now
And you laugh
Like you can't help it,
Like you're finally bowing
to your own joy.
You still don't know it's the end.
I let you spin me slow,
As though we have endless pages ahead.

I smile at the way your presence rewrote
every tragedy in my bones.

The dance is ending.
I kiss you to leave a trace
That even Death would envy
For this last second, for every second,
I would have danced with you.

If you are to fight anything, *fight getting used to the beauty in front of you.* The view you see every day. The old friend whose face you know better than your own. The song that transports you to another time. The lover you unraveled the mystery of. We tend to lose sight of the miracles closest to us, but the eyes of loss have perfect vision and life isn't meant to be appreciated only after its passing.

Every day, I leave an altar in ink
"I'm a pen in your hand."
I say,
"Use me, Life. Use me."
Every artist knows
Creation is not a hobby,
No number of five-star reviews could replace
The way a poem becomes a North Star
For a wayfaring soul in a storm.
We artists are responsible for stripping away
The armor of the world,
Tenderly grabbing your hand,
Placing it back on your chest and saying,
"*This.* Listen to *this.*"

Forgiveness is The Friend who tenderly squeezes your shoulder as you dig up the bones of your past. As you sit alone in the quiet night and look at all the old resentments and aches and pains. Forgiveness soothes those past hurts, reminding you that which should have broken you is precisely what revealed *your spirit can never be broken.*

Forgiveness is the strongest human act—it isn't a word to peacock so the world thinks that we are whole, that we are evolved, because there are some wounds that may always be tender. But without Forgiveness, we destroy each other.

Forgiveness asks us to slip on the shoes of compassion. Not to surrender our boundaries, but to dig up the most startling bone that we too might be capable of any act in a desperate circumstance or with eyes of ignorance.

Yet, Forgiveness does not play judge and jury, she does not weigh your spirit's merit to see if you are worthy of her. In your darkest hour, Forgiveness is the flame that ignites the heart. Forgiveness melts the bitter shards of ice we have encased our hearts in.

She asks that we turn off the broken record of *what happened* or *what should have happened*, and slowly but surely, courageously step forward and keep greeting the world with that most human magic of ours: *hope.*

Most of us women fear we will be destroyed by our chaos. Will this cry be the time we drown? Will this rage be the time we burn from within? Will this joy be too bright to bear? Our chaos is the pulse and thrum of our magic—they are inseparable. *Our ability to create is directly linked to our potential to destroy.*

We were lost in a dance of silent longing,
swirling in front of each other
like two figurines in a music box
unable to take a step forward
but unwilling to let the song end

I look into their eyes
down
down
down the rabbit hole I fall
Alice in a wonderland of nightmares
grasping their vision to see myself
the white rabbit guides me home
"Close your eyes," he says
that's the only way you'll see
down
down
down
until the illusion bottoms out
It is so quiet here,
at times darker than night
the moments no one claps for
are the hands that shape our lives

I wait
without the weight of waiting
I hope without the long walk of longing
I taste the honey of today on my tongue
without the bitter taste of mourning
dripping down my throat
for a moment past tomorrow
I am pulled into your tides
without drowning,
I am the woman who learned to breathe underwater.

Sometimes, "I love you," is said in the subtlest of ways. When one friend slides dinner over to me and shouts, "Potatoes are not a meal!" Or another friend hands me a book and says, "This will wreck you. You'll love it." When my dad brings me another plant, because even botany can be a bridge of understanding. When my friend gently grabs my hand in a group setting and whispers, "Don't eject from the moment." In all of these little ways, we reveal to people that we see them. We care for them. We know them. What a gift it is, to be truly known—to recognize that *our walls are not other people's to climb, but ours to courageously dismantle.*

Our walls are not other people's to climb,
but ours to courageously dismantle.

Life is an ebb and flow
Of letting in and letting go,
Anchored in an ocean of time,
By those we love along the way.

In Hebrew they say,
"There is nothing so whole as a broken heart."
Why make a villain of each other
when we are all little kids
trying to survive without
falling on the shards of our fractured self?
Let us not drive the glass in further,
but offer a pen and ask,
What character would you like to be written as?

I am still that little girl who climbs trees and talks to roly-polies. She sees dragons in the clouds and kindness in the face of cruelty. I am still that little girl who sleeps with books beneath her pillow, as if she might slip in dreams through the gates of a beloved story. I am still that little girl who talks to Death about how much she loves Life, who tries to grasp the thread of the moment but feels Time tugging at the other end. I am still that little girl who asks too many questions, who collects the puzzle pieces of a person to see how they fit together. I am still that little girl, and every day the woman in me must protect her and mend her wings. Listen deeply enough to hear her song and follow that tune instead of the world's.

Grace is the garden that grows
from a graveyard of lost dreams
grace is the silent invitation
to let winter empty you of the fruit
everyone plucks from your branches
so joy can grow roots from your feet again
grace does not ask you to be unafraid
she knows
bravery can only exist in the face of fear
and I have scarcely seen a bird
learn to trust her own wings
without first falling from a secure branch
grace will slip that backpack of past stones from
    your shoulders
so you can tilt your head toward the sun
and begin again

My pen will not protect you from life,
But let this poem be the balm
That turns your wounds into beauty.

My pen will not stop your heart from splintering,
But let this poem remind you
That *heartbreak* is really just the word for what happens
When Life knows we can stretch to fit more of
the world
Within the shelter of our love

My pen will not stop a bullet,
But let this poem fertilize
The garden that grows over
The shrapnel of our grief.

My pen will not stop your illness,
But let this poem comfort you
In the unseen battle of your cells
So you no longer sit alone
In the center of terrifying possibilities.

My pen will not save the world,
But let this poem capture
The way the Sun grows jealous
Every time your eyes brighten
At the sight of an overlooked miracle

I don't know who you are to me,
the man who broke my heart or brought me peace?
Will you always be the ghost
that haunts my heart in the night?
The yardstick I now measure every man I meet
against . . .
He's funny,
but he doesn't make me laugh like your dad jokes do.
He's present,
but his eyes don't cut through me.
He's handsome,
but his kiss doesn't stop time.
He's smart,
but he doesn't flip my reality in one sentence.
I don't know who you are to me,
friend sounds like a fog we wrap ourselves in
to avoid the unanswered questions
and *lover* is no longer true . . .
I don't know who you are to me,
I don't know if I ever will know,
I don't know if you ever want to.

My best friend describes being an artist as, "Holding the floodgates open wide enough for the universe to come through." Every artist has felt that humbling moment when something larger than life pours through their fingertips. It's how I can write for eight hours like it's eight seconds—because love bends time. We know this. The right kiss shatters a thousand clocks. The world dissolves. Creative devotion is the same liberation from the laws of flesh and bone. The worthiest pursuit isn't the work itself, but the way we are remade by the strength it takes to hold the floodgates open.

Delusion is the first step
to making a dream come true.
Wrap your fingers around
the thread of your future
and start weaving.
You don't need their gaze
to give your imagination gravity.
The tapestry of your heart
needs no witness to be true.
limitation is a comforting lie,
when the discomfort of our own power
is what we truly shrink from.
An ocean doesn't seem terrifying
rolled into a single drop,
tell me,
don't you want to swim
in the unseen
magic of possibility?

Silence is my first language
but my second is poetry
yet the most important things
are the hardest to say
I pray you translate the quiet
learn the language of these eyes
because I cannot string together a sentence
that would do the way I see you justice
let's just lie here together
I'll wrap my body around you
like a question mark
and leave the need for answers for tomorrow

Any emotion that goes unclaimed is entombed. An invisible coffin that presses closer each time we cast aside how we feel. Own every feeling. The wicked sense of humor. The irrational grief. The appetite for adventure. The searing desire. The hunger for what has yet to come. The exhaustion when you can't see the way forward. The joy that bubbles up inside your chest. The things you've mastered, and the things you're terribly new at. The longing that tunnels beneath your heart. *Own it all.* Claim every corner of your heart's landscape. Any emotion that goes unclaimed is entombed, but we have held the key in our palms the entire time.

We were two little angels just out of view
trying to help each other walk
through the valley of grief.

I ask my friends to check on you
and pray for you each night,
because I can no longer be there
to care for you as your future wife.

It would have been
our anniversary next month.
And yet nothing ever truly ends, does it?

I hear you in my own laugh now,
in every joke I tell.
I see myself in your eyes,
when you pause to admire
the first rose blossom in spring.

We will never be exes,
only guardian angels
just out of view,
still helping each other walk
through the wild unknown.

Thresholds. Each threshold of terror I cross gives birth to an undiscovered love. I trembled at the thought of public speaking, but stumbling on stage revealed my devotion to poetry. I froze at the sight of the sea, but when the surfboard carried me forward, I discovered a joy as wild and unfiltered as the ocean itself.

It makes me wonder—how many loves still sleep inside us, waiting just beyond Fear's door? The deeper Fear carves into me, the more freedom waits to flood me. One person's threshold is another person's comfort zone. And isn't it beautifully human that we carry keys to each other's locked doors, offering an encouraging hand across the line? Fear is a map. A map to our most unbridled freedom. A map to a love so vast it feels divine.

I hope you see your life for the grand love story that it is. I hope you bathe in the silence of the morning, before the world pierces you with its chaos. I hope you have makeshift meals in candlelight and your home is filled with the deep belly laughter of friends. I hope you allow life to shock you—fall in love with the person you never expected to, move somewhere unfamiliar, pick up the childhood hobby you discarded in the name of practicality. I hope you live a thousand lifetimes within one. Redefine who you are and what you value not on the last day of the year, but with every fresh breath life gives you, because god knows we don't know how many we have. I hope you are gentle with yourself. That you treat failure and heartbreak with the same reverence you do success and falling in love, because it is all a sign of our courage. It is all bringing us closer to what it means to be human. Treat your life as the grand love story that it is, because every mundane and small detail of your life matters. The details are the little notes we contribute to the universe's great symphony. And isn't that the greatest gift of all? *To join the dance.*

The heart doesn't measure love in time, but in resonance. You can sleepwalk through twenty-five years with someone—yet a few short hours with the right person can alter everything. That terrifyingly wonderful feeling of being stripped bare by one who can level us with a single look. The heart recognizes when it's found the answer to a riddle you didn't know you were trying to solve. Resonance thrums on the strings of shock and familiarity. Maybe it lasts a minute. Maybe it lasts a lifetime. But a snapshot in resonance can carry more gravity than a stretch of weightless years.

What if our world didn't condition
us to see aging as a loss of beauty,
but a graduation to finally feeling
at home in the skin we wear?

And perhaps the best way to understand life is to love as many things as possible—to allow our hearts to stretch until they grow beyond our walls of convenience. The danger of a world built for comfort, is that we begin to choose convenience over love. One of my dear friends taught me the term LAX friends, which essentially means the people you would go out of your way for. Isn't it an honor, after all? To drive your best friend to the airport at six a.m. and wave goodbye. To bring them soup when they are sick. To let them stay on your couch when they're heartbroken. To celebrate them when the dream they've whispered to you for years finally comes true. *Isn't it an honor to be inconvenienced by the people we only have so many hours with?* Life changes in the blink of an eye. We move, we get married, we get a new job, we have kids, someone dies. Each season we are in feels like its own little eternity that will stretch on forever, but it won't. Everything we love, we eventually have to let go of when it is time. I'm not interested in the grass being greener elsewhere, I'm interested in planting both feet on the ground so I can cherish every hilarious and mundane moment I have with my people.

Glimpses. They're what we have as writers. The world is a blur of glimpses. A boy with bleached hair journals on the subway, knees tucked into his chest like he could disappear into his own words. A group of kids play in the park, a little princess with a hand on her hip leading them all. A French waiter with eyes like two dark wells of sorrow asks if we need anything—fall into that well for a split second but ask for coffee. Glimpses. So many glimpses of people I'll never know. People I can only love for a moment, by pressing their glimpse between the pages like a flower before it wilts—a petal of their essence preserved.

Toboggans. When I think about what it means to be a woman, I think of toboggans. My Grams came into the house one day carrying four of them. She was the type of woman who had her pearls polished and poker cards ready.

August meant rattlesnakes and blistering sun, but we hiked a steep dirt mountain with the toboggans in tow. She winked at me, then took off down the hill—silver hair flying like a banner of freedom. Somewhere there is footage of three generations of women covered in dirt, howling with laughter and redefining what the word *wild* means.

A woman can grab her toboggan and slide into her emotions without hesitation. Leave claw marks on her insides from all the times she has carved more room for what she loves. Agree to be Death's lover every month. Wear her ball gowns and pearls, then kick off her heels and dance in the mud until her feet are bruised. *Both. All of it. None of it.* We get to choose how many paradoxes we want to embrace—but it is our own courage we ride on.

But for women,
Love is always there.
Her nurturing touch,
Eyes that truly take in what they see,
Ears that hear what isn't said.
When she is full,
Love melts every internal chain,
A balm poured across every invisible wound.
Suddenly the world is brighter.
Suddenly colors are more vivid.
Music is lived in.
When she is empty and tired,
She forgets.
And when she forgets, the world forgets too—
To nurture,
To cherish,
To love.
An atmosphere we only notice when it's gone.

My heart bled for the whole world that night
all at once
all at once
all at once
I watched life unravel before my eyes
I looked down at my phone
and saw the friend who had just died
then looked up and saw
the woman with a swollen belly
waiting to bring life into the world,
her other child jumping rope by the sea with wild curls
that sweet innocence still unbroken
to my left was a man who got down on one knee,
and promised his woman an eternity
to the right
a pianist poured his heart into the keys
with a bittersweet melody
then stopped abruptly
because grief and silence have the same sound

All at once
it was happening *all at once*
each of us trying to be free for a moment

of our fragile human existence
how humbling it is to let it all in
how humbling it is to bow before Life and Death
those twin angels who have loved one another since
the beginning

"What do I do?" I asked my heart, "What do I do
with all of this?"
and I felt an invisible hand reach back
"Come dance with me," I heard.
I danced until my bare feet were raw
and I felt my heart pounding like a drum
I danced until my hair was in knots
and all the old aches and pains had dripped from
my skin
I danced because it was the only sensible thing
left to do in this magical madhouse of existence

To belong is to bow before our smallness. Redwood trees so tall they scrape the sky. The northern lights spilling in ribbons of emerald. A whale the size of a city bus gliding through the tides. Remembering my smallness is not a prison of insignificance, but a doorway to belonging. This world is full of wonder, and by some stroke of luck, my life is a silk thread I get to contribute, weaving into the grander tapestry.

Wildflowers are blooming on the ridge.
That might not sound extraordinary to you,
But I can still see the scorch marks
Where fire tried to swallow this canyon whole

And now—
Wildflowers.

Maybe it's nature's way of saying
There is no rhyme or reason for devastation
But destruction is the fertile soil
Where greater beauty takes root.

Tears of joy carve down my cheeks like twin canyons
of salt.
They call this place a town for hippies
Which is another way of saying
Those of us who are weird enough to try on our
own skin.

I watch the wind snake through the field
Coiling around the brightest petals
A caterpillar inches up my hand

This spotted, furry creature survived, too.
All of us strange, awkward beings forget
To glorify the chrysalis as much as the butterfly
I name him Percy
And wish him luck because I know how violent
And messy transformation can be.
I build Percy a home out of leaves and flowers
For him to safely cocoon unbothered,
And shed without a care in the world for what his
wings will look like.

Every curse has shown me how to break the spell. Every loss has shown me how to love. Every sharp edge I've run into has softened my walls. Every denial has fortified my spirit. I am learning, to bow to the stories I did not write. I am learning, to thank the teachers that wear the face of rejection. I am learning, I am learning, I am

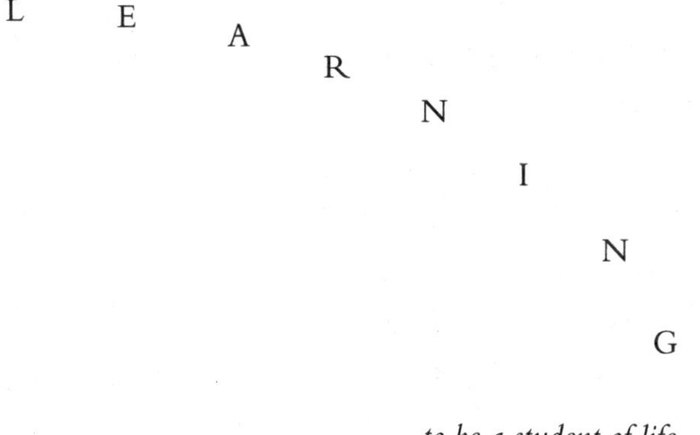

. . . to be a student of life.

On Failure

It has taken a thousand deaths to feel this alive

It has taken a thousand devastations to taste my dreams

It has taken a thousand destructions to reveal what is
indestructible within me

It has taken a thousand broken moments to become
this whole

It wasn't his charm that drew me in,
but the way this gentle giant of a man,
stopped our walk and paused
to hug a lavender bush
alive with honeybees.
As if he forgot I was standing there,
the wild boy in him slipped free.
He nuzzled his chin between their striped bodies
like they were long-lost friends.
Then he picked up a seven-foot snake
and spoke to her like a lover.
I wonder what it's like
to move through life
unruled by fear?
I pointed out a spider on his floor,
and he shrugged—
as if it belonged to the house
as much as he did.

Thump-thump.
Thump-thump.
Thump-thump.
T h u m p . . .

t
H
U
M
P

We are drawn to the people
who embody the parts of ourselves
we've forgotten.

You have to come up with the cleverest things to say
To find someone to be silent with . . .

I crave the raw reality of life like that first gulp of air after being at the bottom of the ocean. Everywhere I turn I see a wax museum. Preservation, but we call it longevity. The choice between succumbing to our wild bodies or displaying ourselves like porcelain. But the flawless rigidity comes at a price—we cannot breathe and be perfect at the same time. *We cannot be loved profoundly until we reveal our true face.*

Is it worth it? To trade resonance for symmetry. Depth for digestibility.

If you've ever watched a child be born or the light leave someone's eyes, you know it's a potent flame that burns through everything we thought was so important. It's *messy*. And yet in those moments, we greet Love stripped of all Her costumes.

True love breaks spells in fairy tales for a reason, and it's not because Prince Charming is such a great kisser. That kind of raw love, that level of *life*, carries the power to shatter a thousand curses.

Her love keeps vigil where your courage sleeps
If her heart is true,
Her love will keep watch,
Like a guardian angel
Walking invisibly beside you
Long after the end.

"If you knew how painful goodbye would be, would you have still said hello?"

"Always."

Being an artist is like walking blindfolded through the world—never seeing the entirety of what's shaping you, only trusting that each sharp edge is carving something true.

We are most dynamic when we boldly walk the tightrope of our contradictions. *The desire to be a good person can stop us from becoming a whole person.* The edges of our core truths stretch wide like a canyon. The desire for freedom against the craving for belonging. The ache for certainty against the pull of the unknown. The yearning for simplicity against the thrill of complexity. Between those edges lies a trench of emotional depth, and I am changed each time I swim through it. When our opposing truths clash, a collision happens. *A collision of aliveness.*

I once had dinner with a Samurai master. “You are a writer,” he said. I nodded. “Your pen is not so different from my sword. But your most honest words have yet to come through you.” I tilted my head. “How will they come through me?” Only then did I notice my fists were clenched. He reached across the table, uncurled my fingers, and smiled. “You just . . . *let go.*”

The path to understanding the universal is often walked in small footprints of the deeply personal.

If I were to describe the country of Switzerland, I would tell you how I could walk alone at night for the first time without fear. The swaying sycamore trees that grow in cloud forests, and the endless stars that blanket them. If I were to describe Death, I would tell you about the way my best friend and I keep her mother alive in every inappropriately timed joke we tell. I could tell you about Life in some vast poetic way, but we are unable to feel each other when we hear of the farthest-reaching star or a foreign land that feels alien. *Poets are magnifying glasses for humanity.*

Distraction is the death of art.
Boredom is the birthplace of it.

Keep the ones you lose alive in your heart. Let their pulse thrum through the ink of your pen as you write them letters. The weight of your world has dissolved and grown wings, leaving the surface of your heart uneven. "I'm sorry for your loss" is our way of saying "Death is too large to grasp, but I am here to catch you as you tumble backward in despair." Death is the one thing all life shares—though we don't arrive there together.

But what if they are still here? What if you spoke to them as you always have, in the quiet of the night? Tell them about the ordinary things. The stranger you met in the grocery store. The joke that made you laugh until your ribs ached. Let their legacy live through you. Let their spirit borrow your eyes, staying a little longer through the window of remembrance. Light a candle. Buy their favorite flowers. Sing their favorite song until your voice cracks. *Celebrate, celebrate, celebrate* the open wound they left! Let it remind you not only that you are human, but what being human truly means.

I never wanted to be a love poet,
there is nothing profound I can say on the subject,
but wait—
look at how his smile lights up the whole sky,
or those deep frown lines when he thinks too much.
Oh no, I'm doing it again.
I'm not a love poet—I swear.
Meanwhile,
a swallow took flight from
the branch of an oak tree at dawn,
spread her wings across
the first beam of sunlight,
and the tree stood there,
his roots holding the world together as he watched
her go.
Oh no, I'm doing it again.
I try to write about Time instead,
but even the ticktock of a clock starts to sound
like a lover's footsteps.
All poems are rivers,
carrying us to the same sea.
I never wanted to be a love poet—
But what better subject is there to be a student of?

Whose body am I searching for in the mirror?
Is it the waist of that girl I saw on a billboard,
or the lips I scrolled past,
puckered like a rose that never wilts?
My whole day is a morning routine
rehearsing perfection with every
beauty tip that tips me over the edge
Quick,
grab the concealer.
Even our makeup is made up of words
that cover our shame.
I laugh at myself,
wearing my denial like foundation,
as though this is the only card I have to wield,
but this isn't even my deck to play.
If beauty is security,
then make me the man of my own life.
Let me build safety with every choice
I make to stay,
Let me embrace every stretch mark
like a comet flying home on my skin.

Stay?
my body asks.
Every day, I have to withdraw my gaze from the world.
Close my eyes and tell her:
Always.

A list of things I'd come back for if I died:

- Swing dancing in the kitchen with my mother to Frank Sinatra.
- Potatoes with rosemary and too much salt.
- Cuddling a sweet dog.
- Floating in the river in Kauai.
- Reading fantasy books while the snow falls.
- Laying my head on his chest for hours, matching his breath.
- Coffee in Tuscany beneath the cypress trees.
- Dancing without mirrors.
- My father's arms.
- Melting in the sun, hot sand clutched in my palm.
- Swimming with whale sharks.
- *The violin, the violin, the violin.*
- Fireflies on a balmy night.
- Reading my goddaughter books, her tiny hand clutching mine.

- My best friend's hyena laughter.
- Writing a poem about someone I love.
- Running barefoot through the jungle.
- Cooking pancakes for dinner.
- The northern lights.
- Galloping on a horse through the open desert.
- Meditation (when I bother to do it).
- Performing a poem spontaneously, relishing in the free fall.
- Playing poker with my grandmother.
- Sitting on top of a sand dune, where silence is the loudest sound.

Listening. A listener doesn't hold you together. They step back, open their arms wide and say: *You can fall apart here.* They do not stitch you up. They lie on the floor beside you, soft gaze saying: *I am here. I am with you.* They do not hand you advice, because they know they are not the one who will live with the consequences of that choice. Instead, they listen with every pore of their body, an anchor in the storm. They do not say: *I will fix this for you.* They say: *I believe, with my whole heart, that you will find a way.* To listen is to let another arrive at their own conclusion, sift through the rubble, and discover for themselves the golden truths buried within.

You do not need to hunt for your purpose,
Snare meaning in every passing sign,
Or make a sport of healing
As if life were the spiritual Olympics.

Where do your eyes go
When you aren't searching?

Do they fall to the first poppy
Blossoming in spring?

Do they follow the painter's hand
As it tells a story without words?
Or lift toward the sky,
Catching the wings of an airplane
And dreaming of the far-reaching corners of the world?

There is no need to claw for destiny.
Close your eyes,
Hold out your palms,
And wait.
Wait for what you love
(and what loves you)
To fall gently into your hands.

I want to elope with my flaws.
Frame the imperfect sentence that is
proof there was a pulse behind the poem.
I want to capture the sound of her
unabashed laughter,
play it on loop in my headphones
to remind myself
we are not polished imitations of humanity.
I want to ride my moods on a swing,
as they lift me toward ecstasy
or bring me to my knees
without trying to freeze myself in motion
and place a filter over my faults.
I want to paint his crooked smile,
because symmetry could never tell the full story.
Years from now,
we will dig for imperfections like buried treasure.
Make exhibits of rare details that say,
"I am human."
Years from now,
we'll stop trying to make things better,
and instead make them honest.

Pleasure is not a luxury, but a way of life. *Faster, faster, faster,* the world spins. Get caught in a blur of time, and we can't see what's in front of us. My breath is short. Head throbbing from a fluorescent screen. He grabs my hands, pulling me outside. Feeds me strawberries in the afternoon sun. I taste summer on my tongue. Suddenly I'm folding laundry the same way I write a poem. I'm not cooking dinner, I'm making love. Jazz music blares, and I'm dancing in the shower. The world has stopped spinning, exhaustion no longer lulling me into a slumber. I am awake, eating strawberries, here to tend to my corner of the world. Sensual living is not a luxury, but our way of remaining connected. With pleasure, we are not running out of time—*we are running into it.*

Love is the unabashed permission to live. Fingers interlacing in yours, gently tugging you into the here and now. Deep belly laughter that unwinds a thousand sorrows. Silence between two contented souls. When we're in love, we lean into life itself. We don't just hear a song—it pierces our cells. We don't just listen to stories—we absorb them as road maps of understanding. Roots grow beneath our feet, because reality becomes more beautiful than our dreams. Love is the voice that lulls you out of your urgent life and says, *Hey, isn't it marvelous just to be here?*

I'm sitting at a café in Los Feliz. Curled up in a corner table. I have to write with my back to a wall. Preferably where I can smell the espresso machine. There's a drawer underneath. I open it. *All the letters we never sent.* I read dozens of them. *My best friend is sitting across from me. He has no idea I've been in love with him for ten years.* Another one. *I lost a child this year. I wish I could mail this to her in the other world and tell her she was my reason why.* Love unsent. Grief without a postmark. I close my eyes and swallow the knot in my throat. *What are the words I am keeping locked away?* And it makes me wonder, in another timeline, if there is a version of us who is immeasurably happy because we left everything on the table.

A list of rarities I wish were common:

- People answering "How are you?" without hiding behind "Fine."
- Handwritten letters.
- An open heart led by audacity, not doubt.
- Saying "No." without overexplaining.
- Curiosity that refuses to die, even after decades of knowing someone.
- A human who knows the weight of their own footprint.
- Meteor showers.
- Funerals that celebrate a life as fiercely as they grieve its loss.
- Conflict that sculpts love into something unbreakable.
- Compliments about who a person decided to become.
- Exchanging favorite books before we ask "What do you do?"

- Instead of saying "Let me know if you need anything," showing up before they have to ask.
- The perfect chocolate bar.
- A day with no schedule.
- A book you clutch to your chest like a brand because the words forever marked you.
- Elders who are treated like living libraries, instead of pushed aside.
- Children respected for their innate wisdom.
- Gratitude not just for what we are given, but for what we are denied.
- Singing and dancing and writing poems without needing to be professional at it.

Her daughter and granddaughter stand in my living room. *Alzheimer's.* They say the word softly, like naming it might summon it faster. I know God exists because of the way they love this woman. They celebrate her life while she is still here, cherish her like a living, breathing work of art to stand in awe of every day.

I've spent a lifetime journaling, hoarding my memories. Proof that I existed, because what is legacy if not the fear of death? Maybe I write every detail to outrun oblivion. My biggest fear was losing my memories. Until I met her.

She pats my hand, sunspots scattered across her skin like a galaxy, and says, "There are two certainties in life. One: We are the people we love, not our memories. And two . . ." She leans in and winks. "The best men are found in a library."

It is not my task to pry the heart of a man open,
But to love him by letting him be.
Isn't it an honor?
To stand outside his doors without knocking,
Patient,
Waiting for him to trust you with each room.
Sometimes,
Silence is not indifference,
But a man testing:
Will you listen,
Without using my vulnerability against me?

It is not his task to open the heart of a woman
He does not wish to hold,
To claim intimacy without responsibility.
Sometimes, being a man
Is knowing when not to destroy.
To recognize that her doors were already open,
But crossing the threshold
Before you plan to stay,
Closes the blinds on her trust.

Sometimes, care looks like
Letting go before you let in.

Our wounds are the birthplace of our compassion.

"Very few people have that, you know," she said.
"Have what?" I asked.
"A life that is truly their own."

When a woman enters a house, it becomes a home. The walls lose their hardness. Spices permeate the kitchen, flavored and bold like her spirit. Suddenly there are daisies in the vase. Suddenly the counter is a confessional. Suddenly your shoulders drop, resting in her arms, knowing there is no aspect of you she cannot hold. Suddenly your place in the world is assured, her gaze the only home you could need.

Do not despair about
Who the world wants you to be,
The world was never watching.
Exit stage left
And send away your scripts.
The best lives
Are the ones worth disapproving of—
Footprints in the sand washed away
So no one can follow.
The only thing worse than a mistake,
Is a person too careful to make them.

Beauty is the marriage of terror and courage.
Uncontrolled. Wild. Capable of devastation.
The churning sea.
The night sky swollen with stars colliding.
A prowling jaguar.
A herd of elephants.
A woman who shakes up the slumbering power
inside her
and lets it burst like a tidal wave.

Beauty is a stunning catastrophe to your rigid
sentiments.
A natural disaster of the heart,
A volcano melting your certainty.
She can be so tender it aches
A child's tiny hand grabbing your own.
A loved one at peace on their death bed,
Ready for the final graduation.
The last kiss—two lips shocked with the electricity of
a thousand memories.

What we often call Beauty
is only her reflection in the glass,

A pale photograph of her true face.
Raw Beauty comes with a price:
She is Love unmasked,
Demanding the courage to bear our terror.
What is fear,
If not the rudder directing us toward aliveness?
What is Beauty,
If not the sail carrying us into our greatest love?

How I would paint her absence.

I wouldn't paint her absence.
Not for years.
I would lock a blank canvas in the closet,
Cover it with a black sheet,
In mourning of a life I never had the chance to picture.

In my twenties,
I would catch my reflection in the window
And wonder if our faces still look alike.
We have the same eyes,
This I know.
But do I still laugh like her?
Or has that become a song entirely my own?

In my thirties,
I would open the closet door.
Remove the black sheet and pull
My childhood out of mourning.
Mental illness can be like a knife with amnesia—
It can't remember
Burying itself in your heart,
Yet the damage is still done.

How do you grieve someone who is still alive—
But no longer the person you once loved?

If I were to paint her absence,
It would look like a little girl
With curly brown hair
Trying to grasp a balloon untethered,
The ribbon slipping through her fingertips.

My father's work was his love letter to us,
I used to squint at the sky, point to the aluminum wings
Flying above us and ask,
"Is that the bird that carries him there?"
A foreign land of glittering sand dunes,
Hallways of date trees curled like the shape of a heart.

He'd return with tales of long nights,
Car chases and country border crossings.
It's no wonder I was a travel journalist,
Retracing his steps around the world
To understand how he found his way home.

"My sunshine,"
He'd say to me, when he walked through the door
After twenty hours of travel
Where he spent the whole flight helping attendants
And pilots with their bent spines
And nerve damage
As a little girl,
I wanted him to belong to me
As much as he belonged to the world.

As an adult,
I learned it's never too late
To start reaching for each other.
He comes to every book signing and poetry show
Like it's my first soccer game.
Now, I break things in my house
So he has something to fix.
Now, we have dinner every week.
Listen to Al Green and he tells me stories
The way he did when I was a little girl.

Time can't close a door
That love still knows how to knock on.

Even Life looks over Her shoulder
When my mother walks into a room,
Taking notes on the woman
Whose smile could checkmate the sun for its fire.

I wonder if she's this alive
From defying every ending that has tried to claim her,
Dissolving her story quicker than ink in water.
She didn't receive a head start in life,
But she flew light-years ahead
Riding the wings of her own wit.

At 28, she put herself through art school
Painting a new life for herself—
With two feral girls,
One on each hip—
Our mother lioness.
Most parents tried to tame their children
But she taught us to rip away
The world's cage doors with our teeth.

When I came home crying
From being bullied

Her solution was to paint the pristine white walls
Of our living room
Splattering images of mice and bunnies,
So I'd know imperfection was the only palette
Worth using,
That no masterpiece began
As anything but a perfect mess.
(My father just shook his head
And smiled at his ruined walls.)

She has now traded her pearls
For the roar of her ATV,
Carving circles of joy in her backyard.
She dances in fire ceremonies,
Names the bears and mountain lions who come to visit,
And mothers every young girl
Who needed someone to tell her
Yours is a heart worth holding.
Even the ground longs to feel the joy in her feet.
Even the trees lean in to hear her secrets of growth.
Even Life looks over Her shoulder,
    when my mother walks into a room.

The room is a blur of smiles,
So few of them reach their eyes.
I am here, in the moment—
But there is no one to meet me.

I wonder if social anxiety
Is my spirit taking flight from my body,
A heart that grows wings with every beat
Trying to flutter away from the discomfort
Of longing to belong.

An exchange of résumés and charm,
There is no shame in the game
But I seem to have misplaced my rule book.

They say I'm an introvert,
Maybe it's true.
Maybe I've spent too long talking to trees.
Maybe I've observed people so much
I've forgotten how to converse without turning it into a verse.

Glasses clink. A stranger turns to me.
"What do you do?" he asks.

I smile,
Awkward and unabashed—
But it reaches my eyes.
"I'm a poet," I reply.
"A poet? Do you make money doing that?"
His question may as well replace
    the Star-Spangled Banner,
And I am about to extract myself when I notice
His hand shaking as it cups his drink.

"Do you mind if we quietly stand here for a moment?" I say.
He sighs in relief.
"Please," he replies.
What a gift it is,
To encourage each other
To belong to ourselves in any room.

Let the child in you grieve who they could not be,
before the adult embraces all that they are.

For every text he didn't answer, there was a midnight phone call where she did. Every tear that fell was caught by her smile. And when I told her the story of unworthiness, she burned the pages and taught me to dance around the fire. Behind every whole-hearted woman is a village of women who picked up the pieces of her heart and stitched them back together in a tapestry of love.

The First Artist

Seven seas,
salt and turquoise silk.
The greatest beauty
is found under the surface.

The sound of wings on wind,
a blue jay's call.
The song you can curl up
and rest in.

Trees older than the pyramids,
surviving from letting
storms bend them into something new.

Sand dunes that are never
the same shape twice.
The smallest grain
honored for its role.

Crimson canyons
that are anything but empty—

the deepest fractures
carry the richest beauty.

How did we think
paradise was ever lost,
how do we dream of Mars
like this planet is anything
but heaven?

Mother nature.
The world's first artist
and the only work of art
we are blessed to live inside of.

The ground and sky have switched places,
I am in a free fall
Of stomach-flipping uncertainty
But there is beauty in blind corners
In choosing without the clutter
Of how you thought your life should look.
We say,
"My life is turning upside down,"
But what if it's turning right side up?

The things I worried most about
turned out to matter least.

I feel like Ophelia
Every time I drown my nervous system
With the algorithms of daily living.
A river that freezes—
Then thaws.
Slowly.
By dusk,
I step into the river,
Melt and wade through icy water
To pull her from the current.
I sing Ophelia back to life.
She picks a flower for every time
Fight, flight, or freeze,
Became
Let's just sit in the soft grass and breathe.

My mother sweeps blush
Across my cheeks for the first time
But refuses to cover my freckles.
"We should always be able
to see the stars," she says.
Three mirrors sit side by side by side,
Like she and my sister are letting me in
On a secret initiation to womanhood.
Like maybe,
With the *sweep sweep*
Of a brush I'll become someone new.
I hope we teach our girls
The difference between adornment
And slipping into costume.
She turns me toward the mirror.
"I don't look different," I say.
My mother squeezes my shoulders.
"Beauty is not meant to cover who you are,
but express who you are."

Fall

The equinox has come—
Day and Night
No longer wrestle for Their reign
They sit down for a cup of tea,
Watch the burnished leaves
Be carried away on crisp winds
Because when else do we revere
Decay like we do renewal?

Fog curls over the canyon,
Like a lover wanting to sleep in
For a moment longer

The fig tree hardly seems
Upset at losing her fruit,
Like she can rest without anyone
looking to her for harvest.

Shake up your branches
Until you lose every bright leaf that
Made up your persona for the year.
Only roots grown in darkness
Are strong enough to carry us
Through the changing seasons.

Winter

Death and I kick our feet up on the table,
Listen to the crackle and pop of determined embers,
And watch the snow stick to the ground.
He clasps His hands behind His head,
His sigh fogging up the window.
Even He has permission to rest
On the solstice.

He points to the sunset with a bony fingertip,
Orange light spilling across snow.
Look, He tells me.
The earth is closest to the sun
On the longest night of the year.

I sometimes forget,
That the frost cleanses us
Of our misplaced priorities.
I sometimes forget,
That grief is only ever pointing
To how much we love,
Darkness the kiln
That fortifies our faith.

Send all the Good Girls home,
Join me in the search party
For their boundaries.
Throw their "too much"
And "not enoughs"
On the pyre.
My Ariels, who gave up their voices for love.
Howl with me until you remember
The song that is uniquely yours.

Instead of worrying
If the ground is upset about your footsteps,
If the space in the room is burdened
By you occupying it—
Let your desire paint the roses red
And remind you that life is not so exhausting
When you unfasten your soul from its collar.

We do not need you to be a Good Girl,
And wear your purity like armor.
We are here to love you loudly,
Not politely.
Let the agreeable smile crumble,

And come back home to this body.
Everyone who leaves,
Pushes you into your own arms.
Everyone who stays,
Doesn't give a damn for obedience.

Send all the Good Girls home—
The world is in need of whole women.

A therapist told me
Charm is survival.
Once,
I had to learn to charm a snake.
Survival doesn't always
Look like a scar.
Sometimes,
She's a smile wearing red lipstick,
A dancing girl who knows
How to keep a snake hypnotized.
She knows she can't fall asleep,
Or he'll remember she's prey.
Nothing is lonelier
Than being enigmatic.
Years later that dancing girl is now a woman,
If only she'd turn on the light,
She'd see the snakes are gone,
There is only her own shadow dancing on the wall.

I want to write a poem
Without a silver lining.
Sink to the sea floor,
And learn to be comfortable
In the cold, dark trench of grief.

What use am I,
When I'm not a broken record of hope
Stuck on a high note?

What function do I have,
When I'm not turning pain into beauty?
Polishing every shard I step on into sea glass.

I wonder what truth
Would pour from my mouth
If it didn't end with,
"But here's what I learned."

The problem with being told
you're wise beyond your years
Is that you stop making mistakes—
You just go beyond your years.

I want to write a poem
With a silhouette lining.
Let the outline of loss
Be all that needs to be witnessed . . .

____

____

____

Spring

I hear them first—
the sparrows singing.
Light spears my lids,
I open them slowly
squinting at the sun.

I rise to my feet,
like Persephone returning
to see the first flower bloom.
There is still frost on the petals of a rose.

I feel my heart thawing.
This day, I clung to all winter.

Butterflies migrate,
I hope they remember
to thank their old selves.
The caterpillar who fought its way
from the chrysalis
to feel the first warm breeze of spring.

Now your ideas are sprouting like stubborn seeds
That refused to yield to frozen ground.
Let decay be the fertilizer you blossom from.
Don't forget,
To notice that you are standing inside of a dream
That kept you warm all winter.

Summer

The Sun drops His shoulders and
S
I
G
H
S

These long days feel like
Cupping light in my palms.
I raise my hands and drink,
Let it wash away the seasons
That came before.
No memory is a good enough thief
To steal your joy.
Salt water washes the past away.

I am nowhere—
N O W   H E R E
The present moment a run-on sentence.
Four hours in the sand feels like four seconds.
His lazy laughter a sound

I will remember
Even in the next life.

If there is no guarantee I will live beyond the hour,
Then how will I live?
Slow and bright as a summer day,
Without fear.

"All great writers are rebelling against something. *What are you rebelling against?*" he asks. There is only one honest answer.

"The way our world has forgotten how to fight for love."

If virtues were s o u n d s
grace:
my mother's voice.
forgiveness:
grains of sand rolling on the shore that were once
 a mountain.
courage:
he defended her when she wasn't in the room, instead
 of falsely bonding at her expense.
truth:

hope:
robins singing to each other at dawn, "we survived
 the night."
wisdom:
my grandmother's last laugh.
integrity:
the hum of the cello, unmistakable gravity.
compassion:
the stream that flows no matter how many drink
 from her.

Some of us outrun conflict
Like a wolf is hunting us,
Closing in through the pines.
One-two. One-two.
Our feet carry us away from discomfort,
After all—
There are so many paths
We could take instead,
Why face the hunter?

Some of us run into conflict,
Words cocked like a gun
Ready to fire on sight.
If there is a winner in communication,
We're all dead on arrival.

Intimacy is born
When we greet each other's
Little monsters and say,
"You don't need to hide under the bed,
There is room for you here."
Intimacy grows legs,
When we surrender our defenses,

our eyes absorbing them with total presence
the way soil drinks in rain,
we are all just looking for a soft place to land.

And still,
We forget that love is slow work,
Convenience, the loss of loving people long term.

Only true love knows
the relief and terror of being revealed—
buried within all of us
is a miracle we cannot uncover alone.
Someone must brave the labyrinth of our soul
and return carrying our miracle.
Only true love dares to wander
the maze of our darkness,
Only true love is curious enough
to spend a lifetime
unraveling our mystery.
Only true love knows
the nearness of understanding,
and there is no nearness greater
than being revealed.

I put pen to paper
The way I let my knees hit the floor in prayer.
Head bowed,
Palms empty,
Heart spilled open.

People ask if writing brings me joy,
And I say having written does.

I finish the book,
Zip up my suitcase,
And leave with a self-assured peace
That the creative well is empty.
That was my bottom, I say.
I'm done now, I say.

I'm standing in the heart of Florence
There is a statue of Mary Magdalene,
Her far-off gaze seeing to the hidden corners of
the world.
The rusted plaque says
Someone spent thirty years carving her likeness.
When he died,

His student spent another twenty years on it.
Two lifetimes dedicated to a singular work of art,
And six hundred years later
A girl who writes poems on the internet
Realizes the most frightening and exciting truth:
There is no bottom.
The creative well is never empty.
We artists are never done.

Later that evening,
I open my laptop
A silent vow to trade
instant gratification
For long-term gravity,
And plunge into the bottomless well.

"Do you think I can hold you down through anything?" he asked.

"I know you can," I said. "But I don't think you can let me go through anything."

Your body is the only house of worship I need.

People talk about time and space
As if they can be measured.
But how do you measure the way
Two bodies are pressed together
And still worlds apart?
How do you weigh
The way our love still grows
After someone's in the ground?
Is there a yardstick that can tell me
Why my goddaughter's tiny palm
Holds the universe?
The most precious things,
Are the hardest to explain.
I'm only a poet
Without a hypothesis
But maybe that is our function—
Measuring the immeasurable with every poem,
Shrinking heaven into a wildflower you can hold,
Traveling the whole galaxy with a single look into
his eyes.
Trying to find an antidote to despair
By reminding us God speaks through
The smallest details.

In Spain,
There is a sacred walk:
Camino de Santiago.
For centuries,
Pilgrims have placed one foot in front of the other
Through dust, rain, and harsh mountain wind,
Until hundreds of miles lay behind them,
Marked by their determined footprints.

I once dreamed I'd walk this path
with the love of my life.
A rite of passage we would pass through
To strengthen our bond,
But I was waiting for him to offer a hand
When all I needed was my own two feet.

Now, I am stepping up as the love of my life.
Now, I am making all my crossings.
Now, I am lighting every candle in the house.
Now, I am free of the weight of waiting.
Now, I have found my *Santiago.*

All we ever have is now.
Now, *go find your Santiago.*

Confidence isn't a lifted chin
And a straight spine,
But the moment we decide
We have nothing to hide.

Wrap humility around you
Like a lover's embrace,
The only assurance you need
Is the earth that never fails
To hold you up.

Rejection can't shatter
What you have already
Embraced in yourself.

My confidence grows
Every time I fail upwards
Because the moment I stop
Trying to hold myself together
My soul remembers how.

Slip out of the roles
The world validates you for
Before they become golden handcuffs.

Break the chains of every story
That told you what makes you worthwhile.

What is confidence,
If not the total risk of arriving as you are?

Staying beyond the expiration date
Is a subtle death that happens slowly.
The color drains from the world.
We grow weary,
Denial costs more energy than climbing Everest.

This is it? we ask, looking around at our lives.
Distraction delays what we pretend not to know,
But it can never replace
The fulfillment of a soul-rich life.

Every day, we slip on the old snakeskin
That has already been shed and tell ourselves,
This fits! It does! See?
The clock ticks,
The years go on.
Until we realize we don't have forever.

Life sends reminders,
The ones who live the way we secretly long to.
There's a fire in their eyes that shouts,
This is it!

Suddenly,
The cost of wearing that old snakeskin
Outweighs the risk of shedding it.
Suddenly,
The fear of never knowing
What it means to go all the way
Is greater than the fear
Of losing what we've known.
This is it?
This is it!

I never believed in miracles
Until I saw the way you love.
A miracle is divinity
manifesting into ordinary human affairs.
Being with you feels like cheating on everyone
I once promised to be.

She peels the orange while we sit
on the edge of the mountain,
Feet swinging like we're in grade school,
I watch her pull the tangy sun apart,
Each slice a confession in her hands.

"I've loved the same man for ten years,
But we'll never be together,"
She says.
"Why does every woman's heart have a ghost she can't
shake?" I ask.
She hands me a slice of the orange,
"Isn't life juicier for having known them?"
I hold the sun in my hand,
Think of the pain born from our hours of beauty,
And say, "Every time."

The only way I can tell him I miss him is my silence.

They call him
The Guardian of the Golden Gate Bridge
His wings are invisible,
But he spends his days
Keeping people from trying to fly.
Kevin Briggs.
He's stopped more than two hundred souls
From stepping off the edge of this world.
Two hundred,
Each with their own life
As haunted and beautiful as your own.
Two hundred hearts that would have stopped beating
If not for this man offering them
Another kind of leap,
The faith to stay.
"How do you do it?" people ask him.
"How do you stop them from jumping?"
"I listen," He replies.

Look how far I can run!
My younger self pants.

Do you see how deeply I can root?
My older self replies.

Look at all the new things I'm seeing!
My younger self cheers.

Isn't it beautiful—what's right in front of us?
My older self replies.

I wonder how it will all work out,
My younger self says.
What a gift, to wonder,
My older self smiles.

Writers live like submarines,
Floating in the quiet, dark waters
Of intuition.
They say we live twice—
First for our experience,
Then to collect moments
Like seashells that still sing
Of the ocean they came from.

I grew comfortable
Watching from the window,
Submerged beneath the chaos.
But if I am safe behind the glass,
My words become untouchable.

Break the glass.
Get tossed around by the waves,
Gulp down a mouthful of saltwater,
And then *look up.*
Look at the stars eddying just for you.

Break the glass,
Now there are things to write about.

Break the glass,
I am getting gorgeously banged up by life.
Break the glass,
I am not watching through windows,
As if I were meant to observe
The divine mess of being alive
Instead of participating in it.
Break your glass.

I'm in the library.
An older woman in a fuzzy pillbox hat
Is reading *Alice's Adventures in Wonderland*,
Red lips curved into a smile,
Like she is no stranger to the rabbit hole.

The librarian asks what she's all dressed up for,
"Life, of course."
Of course.
What isn't there to dress up for?
She notices me staring and winks,
Tosses the book my way and says,
"Every woman is their own myth maker."

She tells me she's reinvented
Herself so many times
Her body is her only mailing address.
That when we fixate too much
On the ground
Our lives will earthquake
Until we remember to look up.

God spoke to me through
A woman in a fuzzy pillbox hat this morning,
And it was so absurd I almost didn't recognize Her.
I almost forgot to step outside of myself
And remember there is nothing in existence
Her arms don't wrap around.

Your heart still beats even as it breaks.

"I have to keep hoping,"
My best friend says.
"I could meet the love of my life tomorrow."
His heart has just shattered on the floor
Like a mirror with too many shards
For the love he's spent years
Trying to glue back together.
We do our best to keep him
from stepping on the glass.

The next day,
A man with crushing blue eyes,
Clear as Sardinia's waters,
Walks into his life.
Eyes you could drown in,
But I have a feeling,
My best friend will swim better this time.

The years pass
As everything tries to rip them apart
Country borders,
Oceans,
Pandemics,

They wait for a card to turn green,
The green light for their right
To love each other without reprimand.

I watch him kiss the screen of his phone every day,
Moje Serce,
My heart.
While they are apart,
He secretly learns Polish so he can speak
His heart's mother tongue,
To offer him a slice of home after he
Crosses the border
To build a new life.
I've never seen a braver gamble,
But I'd bet every cent I had
On their love.

Now,
I will watch them stand at the altar
They built with bare hands
That no force was capable of breaking.
Two men who redefined hope and proved
All it takes to move a mountain
Is two hearts that are willing.

They've forever ruined my standards,
But for now I'll stand here
And find the greatest honor imaginable
In watching them say,
"I do."

Reparenting myself
Looks less like fixing broken pieces
And more like rolling around in the grass,
Picking tomatoes from a garden,
And laughing ten pitches above politeness.

Sometimes,
Our inner child just needs to know
We will prioritize them,
Instead of drowning out their voice
with distraction.

I started cradling my shame,
Singing a lullaby to her
Until she remembered she's sacred.
I started rocking my fear back and forth,
Kissing his forehead and saying,
My shoulders are not made of paper anymore,
I can carry you now.

The path to wholeness
Looks a lot like failing upwards
Mud on my face,

Grinning ear to ear,
Hair as unruly as I once was.

Enough of this fixing,
Life is one long playdate.
Won't you join me?

"You've survived so much," I tell her.
"It makes life all the sweeter," she replies.

A liberated spirit knows
They are a lightning rod,
A conduit for divine electricity
To move through.

They neither deny the power they wield
Nor mistake themselves as that power.

A liberated spirit knows,
To block or hoard
The current that moves through them,
Is to burn.

When we stop trying to own the electricity,
We learn how to conduct it.
When we remember we are the rod,
Not the lightning,
Humility becomes the art
Of being struck by life
Without being burned.

This morning,
My dreams arrived
Like birds who know
Their nest is ready.

I prepared for them all year,
Twig by twig,
Carefully crafting a home
For their arrival.

I did not know when they would come,
Only that each day
Was an opportunity to add more beauty
A leaf, a flower, a blade of grass—
My love is woven into every inch
Of their home.

Most of us say,
First they arrive,
And then I will build.

But the unseen is the only place
Our potential can breathe.
Even dreams are looking for a home to nest in.

When I die,
I hope people describe
My life with one word:
Reverence.

It may not seem dire,
Reminding us all
Of the world's wonder,
But I wonder
If awe is precisely what's missing.

If at our best,
A poet is like a first responder
For the human spirit,
Tending to apathy
With the same urgency
As they would a bullet wound.

There are days I forget my own awe,
When reverence has slipped out the side door.
But when she's there,
I stop consuming because I've bought
Fully into the moment.

I wear my reverence like a cloak in winter,
Instead of praising the earth's beauty
While I bury her with waste.
She is my longest lover,
And only asks to be in loving relationship with me.
I'm still learning how to be a decent steward.

When I remember the impossible miracle
Of a singular human life,
I measure our strength
By how we revere the most vulnerable among us,
Because a forest is only as healthy as its soil.

I'm not doing the best job,
But instead of trying to carry the planet,
I care for my corner of the world.

A world of overwhelm
Has no room for reverence.

But when is enough, *enough*?
When does striving
Become wonder?
I have nothing to add or invent,
I only hope my life serves as a reminder
That life is worth revering.

Audacity. An eviction notice to your doubt. What is doubt, if not faith in what you hope doesn't happen? Audacity treats chance like a game. If she loses, she plays again. If she wins, she is exhilarated by courage. Audacity is not arrogance, but alignment. The privilege of learning the shape of who you are by going over your edge. Audacity moves in when you stop trying to slay the dragon and dare to ride it.

Among all known species,
The world's most precise aerial hunter is the dragonfly.

With near-perfect accuracy,
This delicate insect
Holds the sharpest aim on earth.
More than a shark,
A lion,
Or a hawk.

I wonder,
How many wings do we clip by
Underestimating the power
Of small beauty?

When I'm alone,
There is no border between me
the rock,
the redwood,
and the stream.

When I'm alone,
I'm faceless.
My persona takes the day off,
hangs up her gown,
and sleeps in the grass,
cradled by sunlight.

When I'm alone,
the past exhales.
My ancestors rest their hands
on my shoulders and say,
"Keep going."

When I'm lonely,
My brain claws for dopamine,
As if the double tap of a post
can replace the double beat of this heart.

When I'm lonely,
I'm in a crowded room
watching myself from above,
The applause already fading.

And yet,
I dream of what it's like
To be alone with you.
To carry alone inside of me,
In every room,
Like an inner fire even
The harshest wind can't touch.

You do not need to remember
how to be human.
There is no course, coach or quote that will teach you
the precious ache of being alive.
Don't abandon it.
This world is so l o u d . . .
But I hope you lean into
The irreplaceable silence inside
that is there to remind you:
it is enough.
it is always enough,
just to be here . . .

Anything we bury within ourselves doesn't die—it hides in the shadows, pulling our strings like an invisible puppeteer. Rage denied becomes brittle boundaries, silent in the face of injustice. Grief denied shuts down empathy. Joy denied disconnects from life itself. Suddenly, the world feels miles away. Where is the appetite for life? The fire in our bellies, the joy in our feet, the light in our eyes bright enough to rival a thousand suns?

Chaos is a friend, but if we cage it, it folds inward, a collapsing star devouring the planet of our psyche. The same Chaos that births worlds can also burn them down. What will happen if we stop holding ourselves together so tightly? What if, in letting go, we create space? Like an instrument, emptied of itself, we become a channel. Music can move through us again, and it sings to the bones of humanity. A melody that says, *you are welcome here. All of you is always welcome here.*

Hi, I'm
Allie.
My government name is Alexandra,
which means: *protector of mankind*
my mother obviously had high hopes
for me with that one
but really, my hope is to spend my days lost in nature,
lift a few stones weighing on your chest with my words,
and stretch my heart wide enough to shelter everyone
    I love.
people say when they first meet me I seem shy
but that's far from the truth
I'm gauging how much of my personality
a person can handle while I read them
like my new favorite book
because I think loving people
is the most worthwhile art form there is
my mind is sharper than a dagger
but my heart is so soft
it makes a feather bed feel like stone
I will remember what you wore when we first met
I will remember everything you've ever said
but I'll forget my car keys

my flight time
and if I left the stove on.
Did I leave the stove on?
I can normally be found
inhaling books
dreaming of dragons
or getting on an airplane
so I can finally put my baggage down.
the keys to my heart
are dark chocolate
brutal honesty
and being alone together.
I still hide behind metaphors,
But I love to laugh my way out of the dark
and find great beauty in small moments
My personality is equal parts a cup of tea on a Sunday
    and tornado chasing
because life is most beautiful when it rests
in the dance of opposites
Hi, I'm Allie.

My chest is a hollow cave where you are resting.
When you lose someone you love,
And their body is nowhere to be found,
You carry them everywhere you go.
And so,
I will carry you to watch the hawk spread her wings
    at dusk,
I will carry you down the aisle,
I will carry you to hear my future child's laugh,
I will carry you in every story I tell,
We will find each other
Not just in the next life,
But in every moment of this one.

I hold on to miracles like salt water cupped in my palms. Precious moments in time to ink permanently in memory. My father and I sit on the porch in silence, staring at Orion's Belt. I watch women write poems in eight languages because grief is a universal tongue. My goddaughter and I dance *Swan Lake* in the middle of a restaurant. I pull off a back road in Switzerland to run through a thunderstorm: three rainbows, two bare feet, one wild heart. The miracles slip through our fingers faster than water if we don't notice. And isn't that the point here? Not to add more to life, but to witness what an extraordinary event this all really is.

If Joy finds you—*lean in.* Unlike happiness, Joy doesn't need the world to go her way. She is a result of being directly connected to life itself. Joy is her own wellspring—one that won't freeze in the coldest winter. Joy visits you even in grief—a river running under the frost. Happiness will find you as life happens to you, but joy will stay so long as life happens *through* you.

I watch her surf like it's her first recital,
Her bright pink wetsuit flashing like a flare
So I can always find her.
I stand on the shore and let icy water kiss my toes,
film every time she finds her footing
and howl with pride louder than I should
for every wave caught because her mother isn't here
to do it.

Isn't that what friendship is?
Filling in the blanks of each other's childhood,
gluing our broken pieces with a bond that will
never crack.
I have borrowed her backbone too many times to count
and she has found a soft place to land in my arms
that cradle the girl who grew up at fifteen
Prince Charming never broke our spells,
but we shatter a thousand curses every time we fight for
each other.

They say the earth weighs 13.17 septillion pounds,
but that is nothing compared to the heaviness
I feel on the days of missing you
let this grief become a sanctuary
for every resilient soul who knows
what it means to breathe life into the memory of
their favorite person.
This heart beats for two of us now,
I promise you'll never truly die for as long as I live.

Lift your knees from the ground,
and brave the long walk of longing.
An uncomfortable truth won't clip your wings like
a comfortable lie.

A woman who has not walked through
the forbidden doors within herself
will stumble unwittingly into a gilded cage.
Her nose will not scent the danger cloaked in
sweetness,
her eyes will not see through the desirable mirage,
she will not feel the dull knife of comfort that chips
away at her light.
Instead, she will bloom toward the first ray of
light offered
rather than rest in the esteem of her roots.
there comes a time in every woman's life when
she realizes
she can only keep in check the darkness she admits to,
she can only love the world to the extent
that she has embraced her own wilderness.

Every choice has an echo.

You can only gain what you will one day lose. You can only love what you will eventually let go of. You can only create what can be destroyed. You can only live if you're willing to die—this is the bittersweet trade-off of the human condition. We shake hands with Time and agree to love the world in spite of its impermanence.

A dream coming true means the end of the journey it took to get there. Finding your love comes with the grief that one of the great mysteries of your life has been fulfilled. Releasing your art means it's no longer your foundation to stand on, but the roof that shelters your audience from their internal storms.

The world will change whether we dance on the ashes of who we once were, or feel our spirit slowly decay from a body that is rigidly preserved by indecisiveness. *Every choice has an echo,* and that echo can be music to our ears or a haunting song of regret.

A gray area is never gray when we see with unclouded eyes.
(Situationships)

This generation is becoming attached to
    nonattachment,
the other day I heard a man
talking about a lover he's been seeing for eight months
    and when I said
"How wonderful, you're dating," he said,
"No, no. We're just *connecting.*"
as though refusing to label it would somehow save him
from the potential devastation of caring
as though we, the human race,
are meant to go about life unbothered by each other
and *see what's in flow.*

love isn't meant to be squeezed between business days,
and if you float aimlessly in the sea long enough
you'll drown from a lack of direction.

we call apathy, "independence,"
and burn down white picket fences like never devoting
    yourself to another
is somehow not the opposite pendulum swing from our
    parents' generation
I know I look like just another poet

talking about love who needs to lighten up
but I think the problem is that we don't belong to
each other

what if I took ownership of it all?
what if I said,
"this earth belongs to me
and I will tend to her with the same care
and tenderness as I would my newborn."
what if I said,
"my friends belong to me
and I will care for their dreams like they are my own."
what if I said,
"you all belong to me, and I will embrace you
with the kind of love that can break any spell."
belong to each other
for the few seconds that we're here.
make this life yours
care for it all like it's yours
love it all like it's yours.

A woman has two pairs of eyes
One that truly takes in what they see
Another set hovers above
Watching the world watch her
She is taught young that
she is a thing to behold
A pocket-sized person to carry in your palm
"Isn't she lovely?" they'll say.
Most people have a shadow
But us girls have a spirit trailing outside our shell on
a leash
And womanhood is learning how to rope her in,
inhabit the skin we wear,
And tell that second set of eyes, *You can rest now.*

What a gift it is,
to no longer have it all together.
To sit in our fragile humanity
without the clutter of everything
we tried to earn our right to be here with.

When everything falls apart,
and the castle walls crumble,
we sift through the rubble
and find the pieces that feel honest to rebuild with.

This world is such a mystery,
But I know when the ground trembles beneath me
it is Life's hands shaking up my certainty
because I am never more alive
than when I face that frighteningly wonderful
    unknown.

My heart longs to give everything—
Use my safety nets as gambling chips,
Tip my hat to Fear and say,
"Try me."

There is a little girl with a sharp gaze
Watching behind my eyes,
Pressing her palms against
The glass of my irises
Like she can peer into the future
And make a deal with the unknown.

I tell her,
"Give life your trust
Without waiting for it to prove trustworthy."
Anything less is its own pain—
Like a tree forced not to bear sweet fruit
For the world to bite into.

This pain.
This joy.
This love.
This being human—
We have a right to all of it.

If a father is gravity,
the shoulders that shelter you from the world . . .
then a mother is the atmosphere, the invisible,
tender force that makes it possible for you to breathe.
She holds your world together with selfless hands,
her heart now beating outside of her chest
as she becomes devotion embodied from your
first breath.

Dig your nails into the soil
Of your forgotten self
The version you had to bury
When you were told to keep your hands clean
This world is made up of psyches that have become barren deserts,
longing for the day their shadow is given permission
to grow roots and suck up nectar from the fertile darkness.

I meet a woman who tames wild mustangs.
"How do you earn their trust?" I ask
How do you show them you won't close the fence
Around their spirit and lay claim to their freedom
just so you feel safe you won't be bucked off and broken?
"That's inevitable—the pain of the fall." She laughs.
    "If you want a wild thing to trust you, you just . . ."
She inhales like it's her first breath in the world
"Stand still."

He loved me before I was
the girl in the red dress.
The man who brushed my hair when I had a
    panic attack,
and reminded me to breathe
in . . . and out . . .
he'd say
in . . . and out . . .
out . . . out . . .
out . . .
I had forgotten that part—
to empty out the voices of the world.
He's not here to remind me how to breathe,
But now these lungs are a love letter written by
    every exhale
Because of the way he held my heart.

Every person we meet we silently ask: *will you love me?*
The question lies behind every small action
like a thousand scattered clues we hope someone
will follow
all the way into our hearts,
and yet modern living has convinced us
we don't need each other,
like love isn't as vital as the air we breathe
so we play little games . . .
asking the question in a joke we tell,
a piece of art we make,
the music we listen to,
the success we try to create.

When did love become something we earn?
When did fear start pulling our strings
and warp love into a contest of who cares the least?
When did heartbreak become a shameful thing, instead
of a badge of honor
that we tried for something?
When did we start making a bond of each other?
A successful relationship doesn't mean forever—it *means*
transformation.

Alone is the only time
My heart isn't on loan,
but the only way to escape this life unscathed
Is to never care at all,
so I say to you:
break my heart
break it so wide open
that the whole world can fit in between the pieces.
When did love become something we don't deserve?
When did love become a dirty word?

You don't know the weight of a secret until it's set free

"There's only one way to keep love alive,"
a woman tells me
she wears her wedding ring
the way a warrior sports a shield
that has survived a thousand battles.
they've been married forty-two years
"How?" I ask
She leans in and cups the shell of my ear
like a treasured secret is being passed down to me,
"you have to die a thousand deaths together."

A philosopher told me when we see an animal in
our dreams
It is a fragmented version of us
we repressed so deep
It had no choice but to become
Unrecognizable in order to survive.
From time to time,
I close my eyes and see a kaleidoscope
Of foxes, wolves and dragons.
I wonder how long they've been wandering
The empty dunes of my psyche,
Waiting for me to water them with my courage.
I start with the dragon,
Offer her a drink and ask when she grew fangs.
"The first time we were eaten alive," she replies.
There's relief in her eyes when I finally listen,
She transforms into nine-year-old me
Because there is no cure more universal
Than compassion.

I write as many words as I have breaths in my body,
trying to build a better world with my pen,
because this one is bleeding faster than the ink can
run dry.

A poem for every tragedy my eyes take in,
crack,
crack,
crack,
goes my heart when I see the news.

Holding on to my humanity is a lot like
catching shadows on the wall—
I can only see it when my spirit becomes a flame in the
dark,
Offer a compassionate hand because
all shadows want to know you are a safe light to follow.

I once heard a man's heart cannot be stretched,
    only broken.
It will not bend and open to make room for you
In the same way a woman's will.
We,
Who experience death every month in our bodies,
We,
Who bow to the emotions that rush in like a tidal wave,
Drowning us slowly,
Until we learn to breathe underwater.
But it's no wonder they fear stepping offshore,
When we constantly push the narrative
That legacies must be built.

How many ruins of empires must we stand on
before we realize that love is the only thing that lasts?

This idea of "something better"
Robs us of our depth,
Robs us of our humanity
Until we are merely mirages interacting with
    each other.

Swipe
Swipe
Swipe
Love does not wait for those
Who turn a blind eye until the timing is right.
I once heard that a man's heart cannot be stretched,
Only broken
But I find myself hoping for a world rebuilt
from those beautiful shards.

When I was six, I wanted to be a violinist. I remember being in my school auditorium, staring at the red velvet case and the cream-colored bow string. At thirteen, I fell in love with dance. I was certain this would be my path from the moment I bought my first ballet slippers—to tell a silent story with my body seemed the most wonderful thing in the world. Until my ligament popped out of my knee, and those dreams crashed down like a meteor, but among the wreckage I pulled out an essential truth: the world is not set in stone, and neither are the things we love. We never have enough time with what and who we come to care for.

Death, whether it is of a relationship, a dream, or a body, is the one thing we all share, and has an impersonal way of tapping us. And yet, I still listen to the violin every day as I write. I still put on my slippers and go to dance class. I still tell jokes the way one love taught me and cook curry the way another did. I have too many unlived lives, too many unwalked paths that I grieve and yet, I can't help but think that in some small way, *I am a living, breathing reminder of everything and everyone I have ever loved.*

My mother told me women
wish to be deeply seen,
but she didn't prepare me for a man
who is always watching.

He is my lion in the reeds,
Keeping an eye from afar.
I've trained my ears to hear
Every silent footstep.

His laugh sounds hesitant,
Like he's surprised by his own joy—
It makes me wonder
how often the man whose
shoulders broadened from
carrying impossible standards
gets to be a little kid.

We've memorized our words of farewell,
But our goodbye has started to sound like hello.
I've never fallen in love in a waiting room before,
But every moment was so striking
I forgot what I was waiting for.

His gaze is a gravity
I can't escape or grasp.
But I'd risk the pull of his orbit,
Just to be seen by those eyes
one more time.

"I just . . . want to do it all perfectly," I say. "You'll never walk on water, but you can submerge in the heart of the ocean and see what wonders you might find," she replied.

I want every ending to be met
by a roaring round of applause,
throw the wilted flowers in the air
and stomp your feet in celebration.
Instead of that aching question:
Why did it have to end?
Tilt your head to the sky
and shout
Wasn't it gorgeous?
This isn't goodbye.
Don't say you'll miss me,
or thank me for our time together.
Can't you see?
Those moments are still alive
Before you became a poem
And I became your past.
Let those versions of us keep dancing
Because nothing ever ends—
Least of all love.

My best friend and I lie on the floor,
laughing with delirious exhaustion.
She has spent as much time in the emergency room
As in her living room.

I wish more people saw
How the greatest warriors in life
Rarely wield swords.
They fight an invisible battle in their cells
Hold unyielding hope for every doctor's call,
While they still play make believe with their
four-year-old.

My goddaughter jumps on us and giggles.
"Why are we on the floor?" she asks.
"It's how Auntie Allie gets ideas," I tell her.
She calls me weird,
Then stretches her tiny palms
Toward the sky to catch her dreams.

When I'm away, they read her bedtime stories.
She points to the empty floor and says,
"That's Auntie Allie's spot."

I've never wished to belong anywhere
as much as I do to a four-year-old's carpet.

Her mom and I voice note daily,
Because what greater act of love is there
than to bear witness to ordinary, everyday details?

So I lie on the floor,
and dream of a world where she wakes knowing
the ground is steady beneath her feet.
Where her greatest worry
is how much our little princess laughed that day.
I dream, and I dream, and I dream—
Then catch the idea in my palm
And press it into my chest.

Most people have a therapist,
but I have found the greatest advisor there is.
Who else but Death
can rip away the veil
on how much we love life?
Who else shatters a thousand warped
reflections in a single second?
Forever can exist within the shell of a moment,
but life is only the blink of an eye.
Every step I take
is guided by that bony hand,
so my footprints leave a garden of fertile dreams in
their wake.

I wasn't afraid of him
But the way my body
Relaxed like it had known his touch for lifetimes
Sometimes,
When beauty is dangled in front of us
It's like stepping out of a cave—
You've grown so used to navigating
The lush darkness
Your instinct is to throw up your palm
And cover your eyes
Out of fear the light will scorch you.
It is tender,
This sunshine.
He is tender in the way
A wolf might tend to a garden.
I don't know why it surprises me—
That a man can wield a sword
And shed tears over a sunrise
In the same breath.

The chapel is quiet in a way that makes me want to breathe the moment into my chest and hold it there. Built in 1500s Spain, the walls have listened to hundreds of years' worth of prayers, but I get the feeling we humans still ask for the same things. Light spills through a stained-glass window—one that someone painted with painful precision.

I look up and see sunlight spill through the stained glass, and it feels like the past is bursting through the seams of the present. Like I can feel my entire life crashing into a single second—the way a wave slams into a mountain wall.

I peer into the rich, deep color of the glass, and I understand: our pain, our suffering, the things we survive and come back from—that is what gives the glass its color. That is what allows something beyond pure sunlight to shine through. It creates this wonderful texture, this pattern that tells a story that's never existed before. No story like yours has existed before. This is your time. Your opportunity to add a verse to the Universe's great poem.

Shadows danced across your face in the firelight
You told me stories for a brief forever
And I listened for the honest silence
Between your heartbeats

Part of me knew then,
They were just stories
Grandiose like my fairy tales
A boy who escaped his nightmares
By becoming a dream.

I think of the hours we held when
time wasn't watching,
But after meeting Prince Charming,
I'm certain there is nothing more beautiful than reality.
You were my perfect mirror,
But can you ever touch a reflection?

In America we ask our children,
"What do you want to be when you grow up?"
Not what do you want to *do*,
What do you want to *be*?
We need an easy answer for who to cast you as,
Otherwise you'll be cast away

So cast yourself away,
Gain a law degree and learn the fiddle,
Become a prolific coder and painter,
Flip crypto and quote Shakespeare in the same breath,
Have a voice like a lullaby but speak with words
so honest
They shatter the shells we protect ourselves with.

Show me all the ways
You refused to be typecast by the world.
Show me all the ways
You broke character
And took hold of your own script.
I'll be your first reader,

Eagerly awaiting the pages of a person brave enough
to admit
We're all still figuring out who we want to be when
we grow up.

My father brings me a new plant
Every time I see him
Vines inch across my bookshelves
Wrapping around the corners of my home
In quiet reminder that
His devotion grows with me

To be honest,
It's stressful keeping so many plants alive
But I will turn my thumb green
To have a reason to hold his heart
And speak the language of leaves
If that makes him feel a little more heard.

We only get a handful of hours with each other,
To debate pothos and monsteras
With the same passion I give to Rumi and Hafiz.
The details hardly matter, do they?
It's always the same story—
Just two humans, sharing time together
With gentle care that grows
Steady as vines.

I never loved surfing until a friend pushed me into a wave, and I tumbled into the center of ecstasy and terror. I never loved the violin until I saw a man draw bow to strings in the middle of the sequoias, and a black bear crawled forward to listen. I never loved books until I found my mother lost in one, her mind traveling beyond the edges of reality. That is the gift of love, isn't it? We open each other's worlds. By watching someone embody what they love, we begin to love it. Our hearts stretch an inch further, marked forever by that tender exchange.

Our fear is a map to our freedom,
this morning I let a honeybee land in my palm.
I'm allergic,
but I hold still
because I want to feel what it's like
to move through the world without a worry for
being stung.

What feels so far away
often arrives in the blink of an eye.

Blink,
and I'm taking my first step,
200 muscles working for a single foot forward,
but isn't that the beauty of us?
The way we rehearse the impossible
until it's second nature.

Blink,
and I'm holding a honeybee decades later,
my withered palm lined by a wrinkle for every
adventure.

I no longer wonder if she'll sting me.
Instead, I lose myself in the way weightless wings
carry the burden of such a tiny miracle.

She flies away and disappears into the next flower.
A tear falls as I remember
I always belonged to the garden,
and sometimes,
the distance between
our greatest fear and our greatest love
is only a single blink.

The first thing they taught me in horseback riding was how to fall. If I know how to fall, I won't snap my neck. Imagine, if we were taught to grieve before we were taught to love. If we were taught to breathe before we were taught to fear. It is the ultimate gift—*to know how to fall.* To drag your heart out of the wreckage, dust it off and find a stronger rhythm than before. That sort of resilience teaches us we will not die when life doesn't go our way. It shows us that the monster already chewed us up and spit us out, yet we are still standing. *So what are we so scared of?* Every bruise of failure is proof that we got up and swung back. Boldly. Courageously. Surrender can feel an awful lot like an arm-wrestle with God, but maybe it's meant to be a handshake instead. The deal of being alive is that we will one day die. But if we know how to fall, it will be the ultimate ride.

Some of my greatest blessings
Are the dreams I was denied,
And I'm beginning to think
There is nothing more stifling
To the fire of the human spirit
Than getting everything you want.

He doesn't say, *"I love you,"*
He writes invisible letters with his hands as they roam
over my body,
A goose bump on my skin for every prayer answered,
His touch makes my cells retell the big bang,
A collision of desire and wordless understanding.

In old fairy tales, names are concealed because they hold power. To give someone our true name is a terrifying act of trust—it grants the ability to influence one's heart, to "unname" them. A name has to be earned with great patience, curiosity and endurance. How do we unname each other? By forgetting what a precious gift trust is in the first place. By losing our wonder and our willingness to spend a lifetime learning a person.

It is curiosity that keeps love alive. It is curiosity that allows us to earn a name and truly see each other clearly. It is curiosity that allows us to understand who we love, and love who we have yet to understand.

Maybe you're not tired—
Maybe you need to watch the yolk of the sun
crack open
And spill across the sky in relentless wonder.
Maybe you're not burnt out,
Maybe you only need to taste the sweet tang
of strawberries freshly picked,
Juice dribbling down your chin as you bite
Back into the sweetness of living,
Stomp your feet in soft blades of grass,
dance until your bones sigh in relief,
and yield the weight of living.
Maybe you're not lost,
Maybe you need to lay your head on his chest,
Feel the warmth radiating from his skin like a
second sun.
What is freedom?
The distance between a dream
and my first thought of the day,
The stretch of silence after Fear has whispered in
my ear,
But I don't the let the words sink in,
because my spirit has been let off her leash.

All these simple necessities we call luxuries,
All these reminders that we are human,
The cost of wild beauty
Is the courage to bear our terror.

This could be it. I hear the piano like I came to earth just to listen to the sound. *This could be it.* I send my 599th voice note to my best friend—we haven't missed a day in almost two years. We vow whoever dies last will keep sending updates into the ether. *This could be it.* I listen to the thump-thump of his heart like it's my last chance to hear the song. *This could be it.* I write my book like it's the final conversation with those characters.

This could be it. This could be it. This could be it. The more I repeat the words, the less I wait for life to happen. The more I say them, the more I memorize the footnotes of the people in front of me, praying one day, they will know just how deep the footprints they marked on my heart were. Because one day . . . this will be it. My body will ring out a final note like that violin. But there will be no question that I have loved.

I wish I could live my life in reverse
Make my last breath my first
So I would know what it's worth
I would look at every wrinkle
And wonder how I earned those lines
Who did I love so fully
They made me smile that many times?
What did I weep for losing
That my hair turned colorless and gray?
Did my heart grow this big
Because of how often I let it break?

Now I'm in my nineties
I see my life from my porch
Smell the summer jasmine
And feel my husband's withered palm
Beneath my fingertips
At this point, we read each other's minds
Grateful to be in silence
Still together after all this time

Now I'm in my seventies
I hear the laughter of my grandchildren

they ask me how to be extraordinary and I say,
"Baby find magic in the ordinary
Because the greatest legacy you can leave is love."

Now I'm in my fifties
I braid my child's hair
Just before she walks down the aisle
And I let her go
Trusting that I raised her
To trust herself
I can't protect her from life
But I can teach her how to make a mosaic
from the pieces of every beautiful mistake

Now I'm in my thirties
My wrinkles disappear
I meet the love of my life
The first time our fingers interlace
I would think his skin is the closest
I've come to touching God
We argue over which dish set to buy
And I can't help but laugh at what
A miracle it is to fight over porcelain plates

Now I'm in my twenties
Wearing the confidence of all my years

As I cherish these well-earned days
Enjoying a body without limits
I get to see my parents again
Read poetry to my mother
And bake pumpkin pie with my dad
Knowing there is no better way
To spend my time than that

Now I'm in my teens
Tears roll down my cheeks
As I see everyone my age
Losing days to a screen I want to
shout from the rooftops
"This is it!"
"You're alive!"
Please, just enjoy the ride
Or life will slip through your fingertips

Now I'm a child
Without a single question for
The meaning of life
My laugh can rattle the stars
And I have no thought of the future
Not a single scar
My mother hands me a paintbrush and
 tells me

"The art will always save you
This is how we steal our time back, baby."

Soon I'm taking my first breath
And I hear my father's voice
His hands are the entire universe
And my small body is a world unto itself
He calls me sunshine
And I feel a fire ignite in me
That will never go out

Now I'm in her womb
I hear muffled voices talking to me
And smile
Because I have waited my whole life
To feel my heartbeat for the first time
Isn't it wonderful?
Just to be here
Just now
Just this
Just this

ACKNOWLEDGMENTS

There are not enough pages in the world for me to properly thank everyone who made this book possible. It takes a village to create a work of art and bring it into the world. I feel incredibly humbled and grateful for my village.

Brittany Louks, my manager and oldest friend, you make anything feel possible. Your loyalty, your sharp wit, and your unwavering belief has made so many dreams come true. I'm honored to know you, and to work with you.

Jackson Tilley, thank you for saying *yes*, for making me laugh until I snort on every work call, and for being such a wonderful agent.

Annie Chagnot, I hope you know how rare you are and how much this industry needs a heart like yours. Thank you for believing in this collection, for making it a thousand times better, and for understanding the soul of the poems from day one. I am so happy life brought us together. Cheers to many more books!

The Park Row team, working with you all has been an absolute dream come true. From the cover, to the design, to the edits, to the book itself—these words have been given life because of you. I am incredibly honored to work with you, and to have your fingerprints on my work.

Dakota Adan, you are forever the Rumi to my Shams. The first person I send my work to. My soul companion in this life. Thank you for your brutally honest notes, for your unwavering encouragement, and for letting me blow up your phone with six poems a day.

Jordyn Denning, thank you for saying yes to every wild adventure. So many of these pieces came from our experiences together, and how much I have learned from our friendship. I value your perspective, your heart, and the way you move through the world more than you could ever know. You make the in-between moments worth writing about.

Alexis Ren, it feels strange to write an acknowledgment for the other half of my heart. You are such an integral part of me. Cheers to seventeen years of friendship. Thank you for letting me write so many poems about you over the years. For encouraging my spoken word on the days I'm afraid and vulnerable.

Alex Carson, thank you for every voice note, and for letting me bounce a thousand title ideas off you. So much of you and Leila are in here. I hope it shows you even a fraction of the impact your family has had on me, and how much I cherish every minute we've spent together.

Chelsea Putnam, thank you for lying on the floor with me while I came up with prompts for this book. For bringing endless treats and sitting next to me while I write. You helped me break the barrier for what I normally write about.

Nadia Damaso, thank you for forgiving me when I broke your lamp after running face first into it. (I was too excited after getting an email that this book would officially be published!) I appreciate your endless encouragement, the way you have challenged my writing and my becoming over the years, and that you have shown me the way to complete an impossible journey is one step at a time.

Mom, you are my best friend, my inspiration, and my emblem of courage. One of the greatest blessings of my life has been being your daughter. I love every version of you, and it brings me so much joy to witness your journey through the changing seasons.

Dad, thank you for bringing me too many plants. For being at every book signing, every poetry show. For being the first to order a copy of my book, and for telling me stories every night as a little girl. You sparked my love for books, and now I somehow am the one writing them!

To my readers, *you* are the reason I have gotten to partake in this wild adventure of being a writer. Thank you for every poem you've read, for your love and support—it means more than I could ever say. I hope this book inspires you to light your candles, and that you know you are first in my mind and my heart.